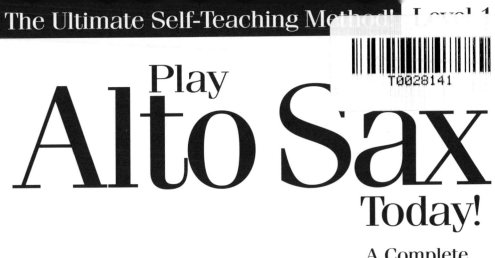

Play Alto Sax Today!

T0028141

A Complete Guide to the Basics

ISBN 0-634-03331-X

HAL•LEONARD® CORPORATION

7777 W. BLUEMOUND RD. P.O. BOX 13819 MILWAUKEE, WI 53213

Visit Hal Leonard Online at
www.halleonard.com

Introduction

Welcome to *Play Alto Sax Today!*—the series designed to prepare you for any style of saxophone playing, from rock to blues to jazz to classical. Whatever your taste in music, *Play Alto Sax Today!* will give you the start you need.

About the CD

It's easy and fun to play sax, and the accompanying CD will make your learning even more enjoyable, as we take you step by step through each lesson and play each song along with a full band. Much as a real lesson, the best way to learn this material is to read and practice a while first on your own, then listen to the CD. With *Play Alto Sax Today!*, you can learn at your own pace. If there is ever something that you don't quite understand the first time through, go back on the CD and listen again. Every musical track has been given a track number, so if you want to practice a song again, you can find it right away.

Contents

The Basics

The Parts of the Saxophone

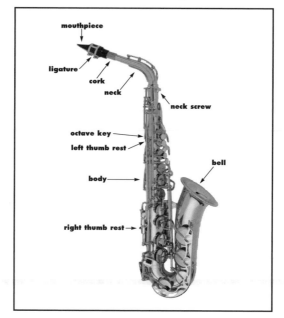

Posture

Whether sitting on the edge of your chair or standing, you should always keep your:

- Spine straight and tall,
- Shoulders back and relaxed, and
- Feet flat on the floor.

Breathing & Air Stream

Breathing is a natural thing we all do constantly, but you must control your breathing while playing the sax. To discover the correct air stream to play your alto sax:

- Place the palm of your hand near your mouth.
- Inhale deeply through the corners of your mouth, keeping your shoulders steady. Your waist should expand like a balloon.
- Whisper "too" as you gradually exhale a stream of air into your palm.

The air you feel is the air stream. It produces sound through the instrument. Your tongue is like a faucet or valve that releases or stops the air stream.

Your First Tone

Your mouth's position on the instrument is called the embouchure *(ahm' bah shure)*. Developing a good embouchure takes time and effort, so carefully follow these beginning steps:

- First place the reed on the mouthpiece.

  Put the thin end of the reed in your mouth to moisten it thoroughly.

  Looking at the flat side of the mouthpiece, the ligature screws extend to your right. Slide the ligature up with your thumb.

  Place the flat side of the moist reed against the opening on the flat side of the mouthpiece. The thin tip of the reed should be almost even with the tip of the mouthpiece (only a hairline of the mouthpiece should be seen above the reed).

  While holding the reed in place with your left thumb, guide the ligature down over the mouthpiece and reed. (If your mouthpiece has two thin lines or grooves around it, position the ligature between these lines.)

  Gently tighten the screws on the ligature.

- Moisten your lips and roll the lower lip over your bottom teeth. About half of the red part of the lower lip should be over the teeth.

- Place the mouthpiece about $1/2$ inch into your mouth with the reed on your lower lip.

- Close your mouth around the mouthpiece like a rubber band. Your upper teeth rest on the top of the mouthpiece and your bottom teeth should gently apply pressure into your bottom lip so that your mouthpiece is being held securely in place.

- The tip of your tongue should be behind your bottom teeth.

- Gently press your tongue forward, but keep the tip behind your bottom teeth. As you do this you will feel the reed touch your tongue about $1/2$ inch back from the tip of the tongue so that no air could escape if you were to blow.

- Simultaneously blow into your instrument as you quickly pull your tongue back from the reed as if whispering "too."

- Keep your air moving at a steady rate of speed, and don't allow your cheeks to puff out as you blow.

- This procedure for beginning a note is called "tonguing," and every note that you play should begin this way for the time being.

Reading Music

Musical sounds are indicated by symbols called **notes** written on a **staff**. Notes come in several forms, but every note indicates **pitch** and **rhythm**.

The Staff

Music Staff

Ledger Lines

The **music staff** has 5 lines and 4 spaces where notes and rests are written.

Ledger lines extend the music staff. Notes on ledger lines can be above or below the staff.

Measures & Bar Lines

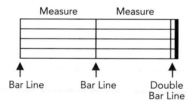

Measure   Measure

Bar Line   Bar Line   Double Bar Line

Bar lines divide the music staff into **measures**.
The **Double Bar** indicates the end of a piece of music.

Treble Clef
(G Clef) indicates the position of note names on a music staff: Second line is G.

Time Signature
indicates how many beats per measure and what kind of note gets one beat.

= **4 beats** per measure
= **Quarter note** gets one beat

Pitch

Pitch (the highness or lowness of a note) is indicated by the horizontal placement of the note on the staff. Notes higher on the staff are higher in pitch; notes lower on the staff are lower in pitch. To name the pitches, we use the first seven letters of the alphabet: A, B, C, D, E, F, and G. The **treble clef** (𝄞) assigns a particular pitch name to each line and space on the staff, centered around the pitch G, located on the second line of the staff. Music for the alto sax is always written in the treble clef. (Some instruments may make use of other clefs, which make the lines and spaces represent different pitches.)

Note Names

Each note is on a line or space of the staff. These note names are indicated by the Treble Clef.

Sharps, Flats, and Naturals

These musical symbols are called accidentals which raise or lower the pitch of a note.

Sharp ♯ raises the note and remains in effect for the entire measure.

Flat ♭ lowers the note and remains in effect for the entire measure.

Natural ♮ cancels a flat (♭) or sharp (♯) and remains in effect for the entire measure.

Rhythm

Rhythm refers to how long, or for how many **beats** a note lasts. The beat is the pulse of music, and like your heartbeat it usually remains very steady. To help keep track of the beats in a piece of music, the staff is divided into **measures**. The **time signature** (numbers such as $\frac{4}{4}$ or $\frac{6}{8}$ at the beginning of the staff) indicates how many beats you will find in each measure. Counting the beats or tapping your foot can help to maintain a steady beat. Tap you foot down on each beat and up on each "&."

$\frac{4}{4}$ Time

Count:	1	&	2	&	3	&	4	&
Tap:	↓	↑	↓	↑	↓	↑	↓	↑

$\frac{4}{4}$ is probably the most common time signature. The **top number** tells you how many beats are in each measure; the **bottom number** tells you what kind of note receives one beat. In $\frac{4}{4}$ time there are four beats in the measure and a **quarter note** (♩ or ↑) equals one beat.

> **4** = **4 beats** per measure
> **4** = **Quarter note** gets one beat

Assembling Your Alto Sax

- Put the thin end of the reed into your mouth to moisten it thoroughly while assembling your instrument. Occasionally rub a small amount of cork grease into the strip of cork around the neck, then wipe the excess off your fingers.

- Hold the body of the sax in your left hand. Many saxophones come with an "end plug" that covers small end of the body of the sax. Take it out and put it aside. You will want to put it back in when you put the instrument away.

- With your right hand, gently twist the neck into the body. Be careful not too squeeze any of the keys tightly or you might bend them. Tighten the neck screw.

- Carefully twist the mouthpiece on the neck so that approximately 1/2 of the cork remains uncovered. Place the reed on the mouthpiece (see "Your First Tone" above).

- Place the neck strap around your neck and attach the hook at the end of the strap to the ring on the back of the sax. Be sure to shorten the strap enough that you can put the mouthpiece into your mouth without having to reach for it.

How to Hold Your Alto Sax

- Place your right thumb under the right thumb rest. This thumb rest should touch your thumb at a point between the knuckle and the thumb nail. Put your left thumb diagonally across the left thumb rest, which looks like a pearl button. Your left thumb should remain on this button at all times.

- The neck strap should support the weight of the instrument. Your thumbs balance the sax so that it stays in the correct position.

- Letting your fingers curve naturally, let the pads of your fingers rest on the keys.

- Hold your instrument as shown:

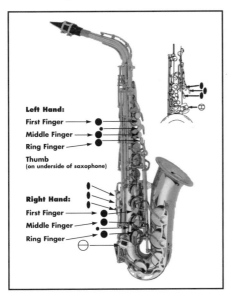

Left Hand:
First Finger
Middle Finger
Ring Finger
Thumb
(on underside of saxophone)

Right Hand:
First Finger
Middle Finger
Ring Finger

Putting Away Your Instrument

- Remove the reed, wipe off excess moisture and return it to the reed case.

- Remove the mouthpiece and wipe the inside with a clean cloth. Once a week, wash the mouthpiece with warm tap water and dry thoroughly.

- Loosen the neck screw, remove the neck and shake out excess moisture. Dry it with the neck cleaner.

- Drop the weight of the chamois or cotton swab into the bell. Pull the swab through the body several times. Replace the end cap and return the instrument to its case.

The First Note: D

To play "D", place your fingers on the keys as shown. The keys that are colored in should be pressed down.

Notes and Rests

Music uses symbols to indicated both the length of sound and of silence. Symbols indicating sound are called **Notes**. Symbols indicating silence are called **Rests**.

Whole Note/Whole Rest

A whole note means to play for four full beats (a complete measure in $\frac{4}{4}$ time). A whole rest means to be silent for four full beats.

Whole note	Half note	Quarter note	Eighth note
o	♩	♩	♪
Whole rest	Half rest	Quarter rest	Eighth rest
▬	▬	𝄽	𝄾

Listen to recorded track on the CD, then play along. Try to match the sound on the recording.

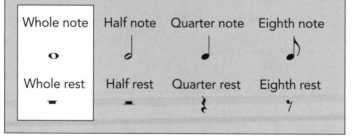

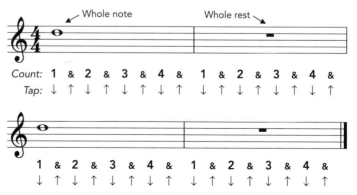

Count and Play

Notes and Rests

Quarter Note/Quarter Rest

A quarter note means to play for one full beat. A quarter rest means to be silent for one full beat. There are four quarter notes or quarter rests in a $\frac{4}{4}$ measure.

Whole note	Half note	Quarter note	Eighth note
o	♩	♩	♪

Whole rest	Half rest	Quarter rest	Eighth rest
▬	▬	𝄽	𝄾

Each note should begin with a quick "tu" to help separate it from the others.

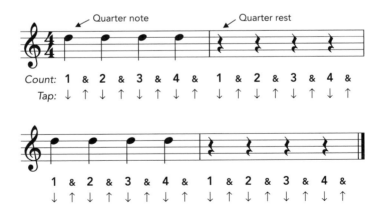

Don't just let the CD play on. Repeat each exercise until you feel comfortable playing it by yourself and with the CD.

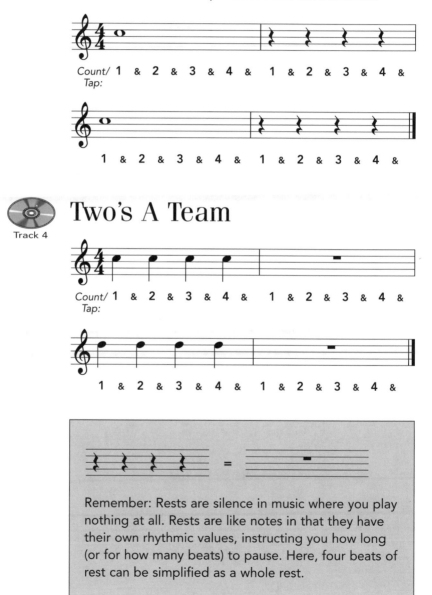

A New Note: C

Look for the fingering diagram under each new note. Practicing long tones like this will help to develop your sound and your breath control, so don't just move on to the next exercise. Repeat each one several times.

Count/
Tap:
1 & 2 & 3 & 4 &   1 & 2 & 3 & 4 &

1 & 2 & 3 & 4 &   1 & 2 & 3 & 4 &

Two's A Team

Track 4

Count/
Tap:
1 & 2 & 3 & 4 &   1 & 2 & 3 & 4 &

1 & 2 & 3 & 4 &   1 & 2 & 3 & 4 &

Remember: Rests are silence in music where you play nothing at all. Rests are like notes in that they have their own rhythmic values, instructing you how long (or for how many beats) to pause. Here, four beats of rest can be simplified as a whole rest.

A New Note: B

Count/ Tap: 1 & 2 & 3 & 4 & 1 & 2 & 3 & 4 &

1 & 2 & 3 & 4 & 1 & 2 & 3 & 4 &

Keeping Time

To keep a steady tempo, try tapping your foot and counting along with each song. In $\frac{4}{4}$ time, tap your foot four times in each measure and count, "1 & 2 & 3 & 4 &." Your foot should touch the floor on the number and come up on the "&." Each number and each "&" should be exactly the same duration, like the ticking of a clock.

Moving On Up

If your embouchure becomes tired, you can still practice by fingering the notes on your instrument and singing the pitches or counting the rhythm out loud.

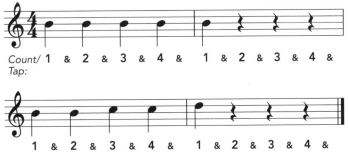

Count/ Tap: 1 & 2 & 3 & 4 & 1 & 2 & 3 & 4 &

1 & 2 & 3 & 4 & 1 & 2 & 3 & 4 &

Track 7

A New Note: A

Count/ 1 & 2 & 3 & 4 & 1 & 2 & 3 & 4 &
Tap:

1 & 2 & 3 & 4 & 1 & 2 & 3 & 4 &

Track 8

Four By Four

Repeat Signs

Repeat signs 𝄆 𝄇 tell you to repeat everything between them. If only the sign on the right appears (:‖), repeat from the beginning of the piece.

Count/ 1 & 2 & 3 & 4 & 1 & 2 & 3 & 4 &
Tap:

Repeat sign ↘

1 & 2 & 3 & 4 & 1 & 2 & 3 & 4 &

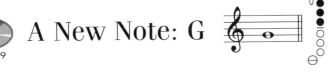

A New Note: G

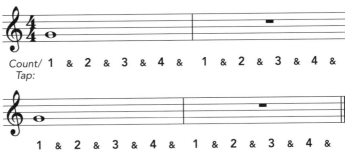

Count/ 1 & 2 & 3 & 4 & 1 & 2 & 3 & 4 &
Tap:

1 & 2 & 3 & 4 & 1 & 2 & 3 & 4 &

The Fab Five

1 & 2 & 3 & 4 & 1 & 2 & 3 & 4 &

1 & 2 & 3 & 4 & 1 & 2 & 3 & 4 &

First Flight

Keep the beat steady by silently counting or tapping while you play.

Rolling Along

Tonguing

To start each note, whisper the syllable "too." Keep the air stream going continuously. If the notes change, be sure to move your fingers quickly so that each note will come out cleanly. When you come to a rest or the end of the song, just stop blowing. Using your tongue to stop the air will cause an abrupt and unpleasant ending of the sound.

- Play long tones to warm up at the beginning of every practice session.
- Tap, count out loud and sing through each exercise with the CD before you play it.
- Play each exercise several times until you feel comfortable with it.

Track 13

Hot Cross Buns

Notes and Rests

Half Note/Half Rest

A half note means to play for two full beats. (It's equal in length to two quarter notes.) A half rest means to be silent for two beats. There are two half notes or half rests in a $\frac{4}{4}$ measure.

Whole note	Half note	Quarter note	Eighth note
o	♩	♩	♪
Whole rest	Half rest	Quarter rest	Eighth rest
▬	▬	𝄽	𝄾

Go Tell Aunt Rhodie

Breath Mark

The breath mark (ɔ) indicates a specific place to inhale. Play the proceeding note for the full length then take a deep, quick breath through your mouth.

Remember to let your upper teeth rest on the topside of the mouthpiece! Make certain that your cheeks don't puff out when you blow.

The Whole Thing

Remember: a whole rest (▬) indicates a whole measure of silence. Note that the whole rest hangs down from the 4th line, whereas the half rest sits on the 3rd line.

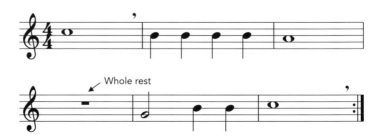

March Steps

Key Signature – G

A *key signature* (the group of sharps or flats before the time signature) tells which notes are played as sharps or flats throughout the entire piece. In this exercise, all the F's are played as F♯. [This is called the *Key of G*.]

Key signature

Lightly Row

Always be sure to check the key signature before starting a new song.

Reaching Higher
(New Note: E)

Fermata

The fermata (⌢) indicates that a note or rest is held somewhat longer than normal.

Fermata

Au Claire De La Lune

Track 20

Twinkle, Twinkle Little Star

- Keep your reed thoroughly moist, even the part that is against the mouthpiece.
- Keep your thumbs in the correct position at all times and your fingers resting lightly on the pearls of the keys.
- Keep your chin pointed downward and your throat open and free from tension.

Track 21

Reaching Higher (New Note: F♯)

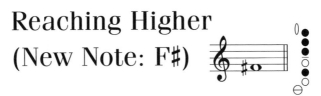

Always practice long tones on each new note.

F♯ (F-sharp)

Track 22

Doodle All Day

Breath Support

In order to play in tune and with a full, beautiful tone, it is necessary to breathe properly and control the air as you play. Quickly take the breath in through your mouth all the way to the bottom of your lungs. Then tighten your stomach muscles and push the air quickly through the alto sax, controlling the air with your lips. Practice this by forming your lips as you do when you play and then blowing against your hand. If the air is cool, you are doing it correctly. If the air is warm, tighten the lips and make the air stream smaller. Keep the air stream moving fast at all times, especially as you begin to run out of air. Practice blowing against your hand and see how long you can keep the air going. Work to keep the air stream cool and steady from beginning to end.

Now try this with your alto sax. Select a note that is comfortable to play and see how long you can hold it. Listen carefully to yourself to see if the tone gets louder or softer, changes pitch slightly, or if the quality of the tone changes. Do this a few times every time you practice, trying to hold the note a little longer each time and maintain a good sound.

Jingle Bells

Dynamics

Dynamics refer to how loud or soft the music is. Traditionally, many musical terms (including dynamic markings) are called by their Italian names:

f	forte *(four' tay)*	loud
mf	mezzo forte *(met' zoh four' tay)*	moderately loud
p	piano *(pee ahn' oh)*	soft

Producing a louder sound requires more air, but you should use full breath support at all dynamic levels.

My Dreydl

Pick-up Notes

Sometimes there are notes that come before the first full measure. They are called *pick-up notes*. Often, when a song begins with a pick-up measure, the note's value (in beats) is subtracted from the last measure. To play this song with a one beat pick-up, you count "1, 2, 3" and start playing on beat 4.

One-beat pick-up note

mf

p

f

Last measure has 3 beats, not 4

Eighth Note Jam

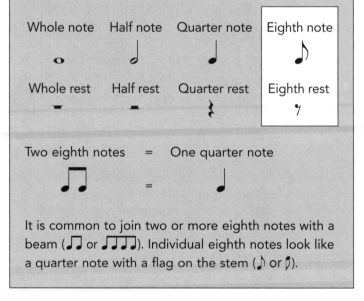

Notes and Rests

Eighth Note/Eighth Rest

An eighth note half the value of a quarter note, that is, half a beat. A eighth rest means to be silent for half a beat. There are eight eighth notes or eight eighth rests in a $\frac{4}{4}$ measure.

Whole note	Half note	Quarter note	Eighth note
o	♩	♩	♪

Whole rest	Half rest	Quarter rest	Eighth rest
▬	▬	𝄽	𝄾

Two eighth notes = One quarter note

It is common to join two or more eighth notes with a beam (♫ or ♬). Individual eighth notes look like a quarter note with a flag on the stem (♪ or 𝅘𝅥𝅮).

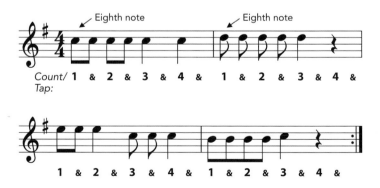

Eighth note   Eighth note

Count/ **1** & **2** & **3** & **4** &   **1** & **2** & **3** & **4** &
Tap:

1 & **2** & **3** & **4** &   **1** & **2** & **3** & **4** &

Eighth Note Counting

The first eighth note comes on "1" as your foot taps the floor. The second happens as your foot moves up on "&." The third is on "2" and the fourth is on the next "&" and so forth. Remember to count and tap in a steady and even manner, like the ticking of a clock.

Track 26

Skip To My Lou

Keep your fingers resting lightly on the keys and curved comfortably.

Track 27

Long, Long Ago

Good posture will improve your sound.

Oh, Susanna

Notice the pick-up notes.

William Tell

- Use plenty of air and keep it moving *through* the saxophone. Blow enough air through the instrument to get a full tone. Compare your tone to the recording.

- Let your body support the weight of the instrument with the neck strap. Don't try to lift the sax with your right thumb. Your thumbs should *balance* the sax.

Track 30

Two By Two

$\frac{2}{4}$ Time

A time signature of $\frac{2}{4}$ means that a quarter note gets one beat, but there are only two beats in a measure.

Count/Tap: **1** & **2** & **1** & **2** & **1** & **2** & **1** & **2** &

1 & **2** & **1** & **2** & **1** & **2** & **1** & **2** &

Tempo Markings

The speed or pace of music is called **tempo**. Tempo markings are usually written above the staff. Many of these terms come from the Italian.

Allegro   *(ah lay' grow)*   Fast tempo

Moderato *(mah der ah' tow)* Medium or moderate tempo

Andante   *(ahn dahn' tay)*   Slower "walking" tempo

Track 31

High School Cadets March

Allegro

Track 32

Hey, Ho! Nobody's Home
(New Note: E)

Moderato

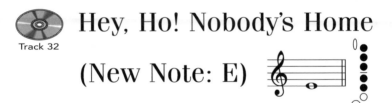

Octaves

Notes that have the same name but are eight notes higher or lower are called **octaves**. You already knew how to play an E, but this new E is one octave lower. When using the "octave key" with your left thumb, just roll the left edge of your thumb onto the octave key. Make sure your thumb is still partially on the pearl thumb button. Practice playing both E's one after the other like this:

The lower notes will be played more easily if you loosen your throat and relax your lips slightly.

Track 33

Play The Dynamics

Dynamics

Gradual changes in volume are indicated by these symbols:

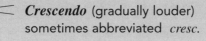

Crescendo (gradually louder)
sometimes abbreviated *cresc.*

Decrescendo or *Diminuendo* (gradually softer)
sometimes abbreviated *dim.*

Remember to keep the air stream moving fast both as you get louder by gradually using more air on the crescendo, and as you get softer by gradually using less air on the decrescendo.

Track 34

Aura Lee

Track 35

Frère Jacques

Hard Rock Blues

Posture

Good body posture will allow you to take in a full, deep breath and control the air better as you play. Sit or stand with your spine straight and tall. Your shoulders should be back and relaxed. Think about your posture as you begin playing and check it several times while playing.

Track 37

Alouette

Tie

A *tie* is a curved line connecting two notes of the same pitch. It indicates that instead of playing both notes, you play the first note and hold it for the total time value of both notes.

= 2 beats

Tie

Dot

A *dot* adds half the value of the note to which it is attached. A dotted half note (𝅗𝅥.) has a total time value of three beats:

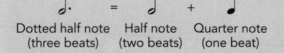

Dotted half note   Half note   Quarter note
 (three beats)   (two beats)   (one beat)

Therefore, a dotted half note has exactly the same value as a half note tied to a quarter note. Playing track 37 again, compare this music to the previous example:

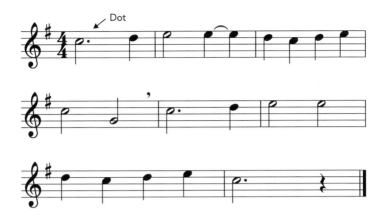

New Directions
(New Note: D)

This D is an octave lower than the D you already know. Once again, practice going from one D to the other. Your left thumb should just roll slightly onto the octave key, just enough to open it when needed.

The Nobles

Ties are useful when you need to extend the value of a note across a bar line. Notice the tie across the bar line between the first and second measure. The D on the third beat is held through the following beats 4 and 1.

Three Beat Jam

$\frac{3}{4}$ Time

The next song is in $\frac{3}{4}$ time signature. That is, three beats (quarter notes) per measure.

Three beats per measure

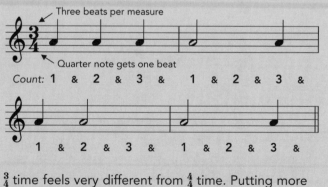

Quarter note gets one beat

Count: 1 & 2 & 3 & 1 & 2 & 3 &

1 & 2 & 3 & 1 & 2 & 3 &

$\frac{3}{4}$ time feels very different from $\frac{4}{4}$ time. Putting more emphasis on the first beat of each measure will help you feel the new meter.

Morning (from Peer Gynt)

Track 41

Andante

p

mf ———————— *p*

Hand and Finger Position

Now is a good time to go back to page 9 and review proper hand and finger position. This is very important to proper technique. Keeping the fingers curved and close to their assigned keys will allow your fingers and hands to be relaxed and will aid in getting from one note to another quickly, easily, and accurately. The further you lift your fingers off the keys, the more likely that you will put them down on the wrong key or not securely close the key. Besides that, fingers pointing in all directions doesn't look good!

- As you finger the notes on your sax, you can practice quietly by speaking the names of the notes, counting out the rhythms, or singing or whistling the pitches.
- Don't let your cheeks puff out when you play.

Track 42

Mexican Clapping Song ("Chiapanecas")

Accent

The accent (>) means you should emphasize the note to which it is attached. Do this by using a more explosive "t" on the "tu" with which you produce the note.

Track 43

Hot Muffins
(New Note: F)

Sharps, Flats, and Naturals

Any sharp (♯), flat (♭), or natural (♮) sign that appears in the music but is not in the key signature is called an *accidental*. The accidental in the next example is an F♮ and it effects all of the F's for the rest of the measure.

A **sharp** (♯) raises the pitch of a note by one half step.

A **flat** (♭) lowers the pitch of a note by one half step.

A **natural** (♮) cancels a previous sharp or flat, returning a note to its original pitch.

When a song requires a note to be a half step higher or lower, you'll see a sharp (♯), flat (♭), or natural (♮) sign in front of it. This tells you to raise or lower the note *for that measure only.* We'll see more of these "accidentals" as we continue learning more notes on the sax.

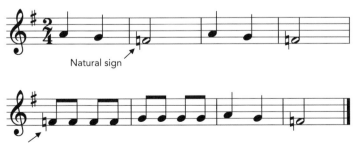

Natural sign

Play all F's in this measure as F♮ (F-naturals).

Cossack Dance

Notice the repeat sign at the end of the fourth measure. Although this particular repeat sign does not occur at the end of the exercise, it behaves just like any other repeat sign. Play the repeated section twice, then continue.

Basic Blues
(New Note: F)

High Flying

Key Signature – C

This exercise introduces a new key signature: the **Key of C**. There are no sharps or flats in this key.

1st and 2nd Endings

The use of *1st and 2nd endings* is a variant on the basic repeat sign. You play through the music to the repeat sign and repeat as always, but the second time through the music, skip the measure or measures under the "first ending" and go directly to the "second ending."

Moderato

mf

Key of C

1st ending   2nd ending

Up On A Housetop

Always check the key signature before you play.

Track 48

The Big Airstream
(New Note: G)

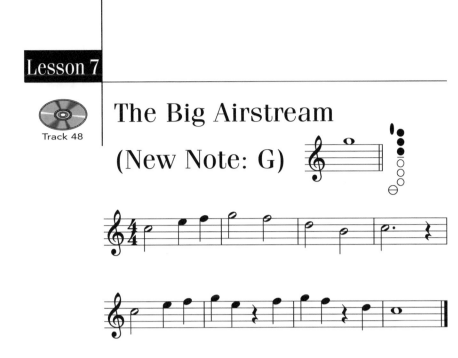

Track 49

Waltz Theme

Moderato

Down By The Station

Track 50

Allegro

Banana Boat Song

Track 51

D.C. al Fine

At the **D.C. al Fine**, play again from the beginning, stopping at **Fine**. D.C. is the abbreviation for Da Capo (dah cah' poh), which means "to the beginning." Fine (fee' neh) means "the end."

Moderato

Fine

D.C. al Fine

Track 52

Razor's Edge
(New Note: C♯)

On the saxophone, this C♯ is played "open," that is, no keys are pressed.

Sharp Sign

A sharp sign (♯) raises the pitch of a note by a half-step for the remainder of the measure.

Sharp sign

Track 53

The Music Box

Moderato

Smooth Operator

Slur

A curved line connecting notes of different pitch is called a **slur**. Notice the difference between a slur and a tie, which connects notes of the **same** pitch.

Only tongue the first note of a slur. As you finger the next note, keep the breath going. You must precisely change the fingering from one note to the next to prevent extraneous pitches from sounding.

Gliding Along

This exercise is almost identical to the previous one. Notice how the different slurs change the tonguing.

Track 56

Take The Lead
(New Note: F#)

Remember to practice the octaves when you learn
a new note.

Track 57

The Cold Wind

Phrase

A phrase is a musical "sentence," often 2 or 4
measures long. Try to play a phrase in one breath.

Phrase

p ——— mf

Phrase

p

Satin Latin

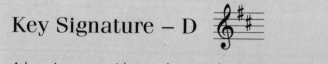

Key Signature – D

A key signature with two sharps indicates that all written F's and C's should be played as F#'s and C#'s. This is the **Key of D**.

Multiple Measure Rest

Sometimes you won't play for several measures. The number above the **multiple measure rest** (▬) indicates how many full measures to rest. Count through the silent measures.

Track 59

March Militaire

Allegro

Track 60

The Flat Zone
(New Note: B♭)

Flat Sign

A flat sign (♭) lowers the pitch of a note by
a half-step for the remainder of the measure.

Learning this note, remember two things. First, keep your
fingertips on the pearls of the keys at all times. Second, just
turn your right hand inward slightly so that you press down
the side B-flat key with the side of your index finger.

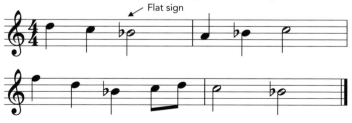

49

On Top Of Old Smokey

Check the key signature.

All Through The Night

Dotted Quarter Note

Remember that a dot adds half the value of the note.
A dotted quarter note followed by a eighth note
(♩. ♪) and (♩ ♪ ♪) have the same rhythmic value.

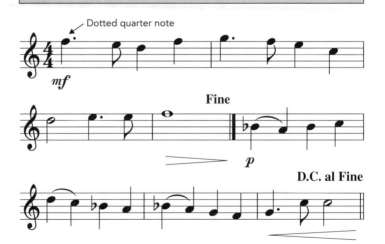

Track 63

Sea Chanty

Always use a full air stream.

Track 64

Scarborough Fair

Auld Lang Syne

- Since lower tones tend to be louder, be sure to work for a smooth, even sound throughout your range.

- Play smoothly and evenly by keeping your fingers close to the keys at all times.

Track 66

Crossing Over (New Note: A)

Track 67

Michael Row The Boat Ashore

Repeat the section of music enclosed by the repeat signs (‖: :‖). If 1st and 2nd endings are used, they are played as usual—but go back only to the first repeat sign, not to the beginning.

Track 68

Botany Bay

Allegro

mf

f

mf

¢ Time Signature

Common time (**¢**) is the same as $\frac{4}{4}$.

Track 69

Finlandia

Andante

Common time

Track 70

When The Saints Go Marching In

Lowland Gorilla Walk
(Alternate fingering: C)

Several notes on the saxophone can be played with more than one fingering. These different fingerings are called "alternate fingerings." When going between this C to the B just below it, it may be easier to use this new fingering.

The Streets of Laredo

Alto Sax Scales and Arpeggios

Key of G

1.

2.

3.

4.

Alto Sax Scales and Arpeggios

Key of C

1.

2.

3.

4.

Alto Sax Scales and Arpeggios

Key of D

1.

2.

3.

4.

Alto Sax Scales and Arpeggios
Key of F

1.

2.

3.

4.

Bonus Songs

The last section of this book features five well-known pop and movie favorites. Before we begin, lets review a few things.

Time Signature

The time signature indicates how many beats there are in a measure, and what kind of note gets one beat. $\frac{4}{4}$ is probably the most common time signature. The **top number** tells you how many beats are in each measure; the **bottom number** tells you what kind of note receives one beat. In $\frac{4}{4}$ time there are four beats in the measure and a **quarter note** ($\downarrow$ or $\uparrow$) equals one beat.

Key Signature

Before playing a song always check the **key signature**. A key signature (the group of flats or sharps before the time signature) tells which noyes are played as flats or sharps throughout the entire piece.

Tempo Markings

The speed or pace of music is called **tempo**. Tempo markings are usually written above the staff. Many of these terms come from the Italian.

Allegro	(ah lay' grow)	Fast tempo
Moderato	(mah der ah' tow)	Medium or moderate tempo
Andante	(ahn dahn' tay)	Slower "walking" tempo

Tempo markings can also describe what style to play a piece of music.

Multiple Measure Rest

Sometimes you won't play for several measures. The number above the **multiple measure rest** (▬) indicates how many full measures to rest. Count through the silent measures.

Dynamics

Dynamics refer to how loud or soft the music is. Traditionally, many musical terms (including dynamic markings) are called by their Italian names:

f	forte *(four' tay)*	loud
mf	mezzo forte *(met' zoh four' tay)*	moderately loud
p	piano *(pee ahn' oh)*	soft

Gradual changes in volume are indicated by these symbols:

Crescendo (gradually louder)
sometimes abbreviated *cresc.*

Decrescendo or *Diminuendo* (gradually softer)
sometimes abbreviated *dim.*

Slur

A curved line connecting notes of different pitch is called a *slur*. Notice the difference between a slur and a tie, which connects notes of the *same* pitch.

Only tongue the first note of a slur. As you finger the next note, keep the breath going. You must precisely change the fingering from one note to the next to prevent extraneous pitches from sounding.

Accent

The accent (>) means you should emphasize the note to which it is attached. Do this by using a more explosive "t" on the "tu" with which you produce the note.

Repeat Signs

Repeat signs tell you to repeat everything between them. If only the sign on the right appears (:‖), repeat from the beginning of the piece.

Fermata

The fermata (⌢) indicates that a note or rest is held somewhat longer than normal.

Now you are ready to play the **bonus songs!**

Track 73

Forrest Gump – Main Title

(Feather Theme)

from the Paramount Motion Picture FORREST GUMP

Music by ALAN SILVESTRI

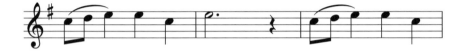

Track 74

We Will Rock You

Words and Music by BRIAN MAY

The Man From Snowy River

Track 75

(Main Title Theme)
from THE MAN FROM SNOWY RIVER

By BRUCE ROWLAND

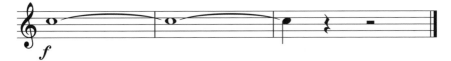

Chariots Of Fire

Track 76

from CHARIOTS OF FIRE

Music by VANGELIS

Track 77

Rock & Roll – Part II
(The Hey Song)

Words and Music by
MIKE LEANDER and GARY GLITTER

Hey!   Huh!   Hey!   Huh!

Hey!   Hey!

ff

Hey!

Hey!

Hey!

Fingering Chart for Alto Sax

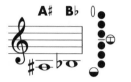 

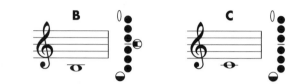

  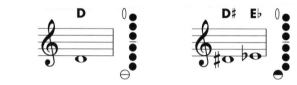

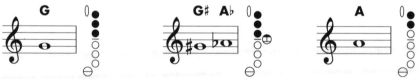

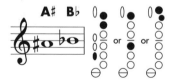 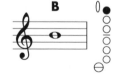

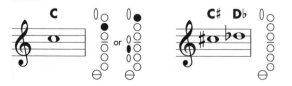 

Fingering Chart for Alto Sax

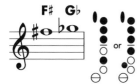

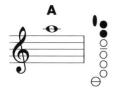

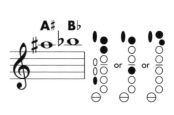

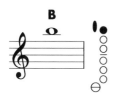

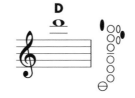

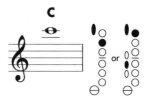

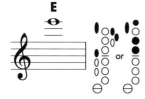

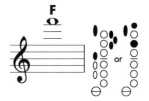

Glossary of Musical Terms

Accent	An Accent mark (>) means you should emphasize the note to which it is attached.
Accidental	Any sharp (♯), flat (♭), or natural (♮) sign that appears in the music but is not in the key signature is called an Accidental.
Allegro	Fast tempo.
Andante	Slower "walking" tempo.
Arpeggio	An Arpeggio is a "broken" chord whose notes are played individually.
Bass Clef (𝄢)	(F Clef) indicates the position of note names on a music staff: The fourth line in Bass Clef is F.
Bar Lines	Bar Lines divide the music staff into measures.
Beat	The Beat is the pulse of music, and like a heartbeat it should remain very steady. Counting aloud and foot-tapping help maintain a steady beat.
Breath Mark	The Breath Mark (ˏ) indicates a specific place to inhale. Play the proceeding note for the full length then take a deep, quick breath through your mouth.
Chord	When two or more notes are played together, they form a Chord or harmony.
Chromatic Notes	Chromatic Notes are altered with sharps, flats and natural signs which are not in the key signature.
Chromatic Scale	The smallest distance between two notes is a half-step, and a scale made up of consecutive half-steps is called a Chromatic Scale.
Common Time	Common Time (𝄴) is the same as $\frac{4}{4}$ time signature.
Crescendo	Play gradually louder. (*cresc.*)
D.C. al Fine	D.C. al Fine means to play again from the beginning, stopping at Fine. D.C. is the abbreviation for Da Capo, or "to the beginning," and Fine means "the end."
Decrescendo	Play gradually softer. (*decresc.*)
Diminuendo	Same as decrescendo. (*dim.*)

Dotted Half Note	A note three beats long in duration ($\d.$). A dot adds half the value of the note.
Dotted Quarter Note	A note one and a half beats long in duration ($\d.$). A dot adds half the value of the note.
Double Bar (‖)	Indicates the end of a piece of music.
Duet	A composition with two different parts played together.
Dynamics	Dynamics indicate how loud or soft to play a passage of music. Remember to use full breath support to control your tone at all dynamic levels.
Eighth Note	An Eighth Note (♪) receives half the value of a quarter note, that is, half a beat. Two or more eighth notes are usually joined together with a beam, like this: ♫
Eighth Rest	Indicates 1/2 beat of silence. (𝄾)
Embouchure	Your mouth's position on the mouthpiece of the instrument.
Enharmonics	Two notes that are written differently, but sound the same (and played with the same fingering) are called Enharmonics.
Fermata	The Fermata (𝄐) indicates that a note (or rest) is held somewhat longer than normal.
1st & 2nd Endings	The use of 1st and 2nd Endings is a variant on the basic repeat sign. You play through the music to the repeat sign and repeat as always, but the second time through the music, skip the measure or measures under the "first ending" and go directly to the "second ending."
Flat (♭)	Lowers the note a half step and remains in effect for the entire measure.
Forte (f)	Play loudly.
Half Note	A Half Note (𝅗𝅥) receives two beats. It's equal in length to two quarter notes.
Half Rest	The Half Rest (▬) marks two beats of silence.

Glossary continued

Harmony	Two or more notes played together. Each combination forms a chord.
Interval	The distance between two pitches is an Interval.
Key Signature	A Key Signature (the group of sharps or flats before the time signature) tells which notes are played as sharps or flats throughout the entire piece.
Largo	Play very slow.
Ledger Lines	Ledger Lines extend the music staff. Notes on ledger lines can be above or below the staff.
Mezzo Forte (mf)	Play moderately loud.
Mezzo Piano (mp)	Play moderately soft.
Moderato	Medium or moderate tempo.
Multiple Measure Rest	The number above the staff tells you how many full measures to rest. Count each measure of rest in sequence. (▐▬▬◀)
Music Staff	The Music Staff has 5 lines and 4 spaces where notes and rests are written.
Natural Sign (♮)	Cancels a flat (♭) or sharp (♯) and remains in effect for the entire measure.
Notes	Notes tell us how high or low to play by their placement on a line or space of the music staff, and how long to play by their shape.
Phrase	A Phrase is a musical "sentence," often 2 or 4 measures long.
Piano (p)	Play soft.
Pitch	The highness or lowness of a note which is indicated by the horizontal placement of the note on the music staff.
Pick-Up Notes	One or more notes that come before the first full measure. The beats of Pick-Up Notes are subtracted from the last measure.
Quarter Note	A Quarter Note (♩) receives one beat. There are 4 quarter notes in a $\frac{4}{4}$ measure.

Quarter Rest	The Quarter Rest (𝄽) marks one beat of silence.
Repeat Sign	The Repeat Sign (:‖) means to play once again from the beginning without pause. Repeat the section of music enclosed by the repeat signs (‖:≡:‖). If 1st and 2nd endings are used, they are played as usual—but go back only to the first repeat sign, not to the beginning.
Rests	Rests tell us to count silent beats.
Rhythm	Rhythm refers to how long, or for how many beats a note lasts.
Scale	A Scale is a sequence of notes in ascending or descending order. Like a musical "ladder," each step is the next consecutive note in the key signature.
Sharp (♯)	Raises the note a half step and remains in effect for the entire measure.
Slur	A curved line connecting notes of different pitch is called a Slur.
Tempo	Tempo is the speed of music.
Tempo Markings	Tempo Markings are usually written above the staff, in Italian. (Allegro, Moderato, Andante)
Tie	A Tie is a curved line connecting two notes of the same pitch. It indicates that instead of playing both notes, you play the first note and hold it for the total time value of both notes.
Time Signature	Indicates how many beats per measure and what kind of note gets one beat.
Treble Clef (𝄞)	(G Clef) indicates the position of note names on a music staff: The second line in Treble Clef is G.
Trio	A Trio is a composition with three parts played together.
Whole Note	A Whole Note (𝅝) lasts for four full beats (a complete measure in $\frac{4}{4}$ time).
Whole Rest	The Whole Rest (▬) indicates a whole measure of silence.